D1300323

PRIME

A full-length comedy in verse by
Ellen Margolis

www.youthplays.com
info@youthplays.com
424-703-5315

CAST OF CHARACTERS

ERDOS, a serious young man.

DAR, female.

DION, male.

These two are royals from adjoining kingdoms who have only met recently. They are dressed simply, prepared for travel. They are excited and nervous about what lies ahead, and coping in their different ways.

CONSTANCE, female.

CORNELIUS, male.

TREY, male.

Constance and Cornelius are sister and brother, close in age. Constance is a little older and more reserved; Cornelius is more emotional and impulsive. He dresses with a sense of style. Trey is not manipulative or a player; he simply falls for both of them.

The Qs:

QUINN, sharp, clever. Smile can be menacing.

QUEENIE , female, large, sexy, charismatic.

QUENTIN

QUEASY

These two are followers, somewhat scary, like henchmen.

QUERY, female, sneaky, expressive, good mover, doesn't speak.

The Qs are hearty, high energy, loud. Cheerful, but with hair-trigger tempers. Costumed like school crossing guards, with sashes of a family tartan if possible, as there is something Scottish about them.

The Seven, from a different land entirely:

ALFA, head of this tribe.

BERNIE, female.

CHARLEY, male.

DELTA, female.

ERNIE

FARLEY

GREG, male.

Characters are all in their teens. Except where specified, actors of any gender, ethnicity, or physical ability may be cast. Family resemblances within groups would be ideal, but costuming can also help establish those connections.

SETTING

A beautiful valley, and the kingdom nearby. All should be created primarily through the imagination. Ladders for trees, etc. Something that suggests a cave for Erdos.

ACKNOWLEDGEMENTS

Prime was originally produced at Woodrow Wilson High School, Portland, Oregon, in February of 2015.

Production Team:
Director and Choreographer: Matthew B. Zrebski; Scenic and PR Design: Jamie M. Miller; Costume and Styling Design: Morgan McFadden; Lighting Design: Jeff Woods; Original Music Composition and Sound Design: Matthew B. Zrebski; Properties Design: Shayla Norris-York and Sofia Vilches; Stage Management: Zoe O'Loughlin.

Cast:

ERDOS	Henry Hakanson
DAR	Elena Braxton
DION	Michel Castillo
CONSTANCE	Sydney Yeargers
CORNELIUS	Luke Burton
TREY	Aidan Sivers-Boyce
QUINN	Guthrie Stafford
QUENTIN	Gwyneth Bushman
QUEASY	Elijah Moon
QUERY	Gracie Dills
QUEENIE	Jenna Hillenbrand
ALFA	Abbey Hanson
BERNIE	Fiona Murphy
CHARLEY	Zachary Johnsen
DELTA	Mattie Richardson
ERNIE	Kyle Turner
FARLEY	Andrew Foran
GREG	Lukas Aberle

Crew:
ASM/Sound Operator: Molly Girsch. ASM/Backstage Lead: Zoe Stuckless. Costume Leads: Kai Clayton, Sarah Hall-Dolezal. Styling Lead: Elizabeth Sikora. Scenic Lead: Emily Coker. Rigging Lead: Mary Michels. Photography: Jenna Hillenbrand, Steve Patterson. Stage and Costume Construction: The WHS Stagecraft/Styling classes.

Dedicated with love to Matt, Jamie, and the original cast and crew.

(Lights up; ERDOS alone at the exact center of the stage.)

ERDOS: A chopstick. A sock.
A pant leg. A glove.
A single kidney, just one lung.
Below without above.

An eyebrow. An antler.
A shoelace. A hand.
A bicycle with just one wheel.
One footprint in the sand.

(Erdos lifts one foot and stands like a stork for a moment, then starts to hop away.)

(A moment later, enter DAR and DION at a run, perhaps from over a hill or rise.)

(Erdos quickly hops away to where he can observe them from a discreet distance.)

DION: You're out of breath. We have to stop someplace.
Let's rest right here.

DAR: But we don't know it's safe!

DION: We've come so far, I'm sure our track's gone stale.
It's getting dark, they must have lost our trail.
Besides, we're not so valuable, your Maj—

DAR: We're royalty! They won't give up so fast.
We have to move. My dad will never quit;
Get up, you know I'm right, no talk, that's it!

(Dar tries to take a few more steps, but nearly faints from exhaustion.)

DION: You're overwhelmed. The journey was too draining.
And look—I'm feeling drops, it's started raining.
Please trust me. Get some sleep now if you can.

DAR: And in the morning?

DION: We'll stick to the plan.
You'll go your own way, find some honest work,

DAR: And you'll go yours and find out what you're worth.

DION: Exactly. If I got the chance, I could
Learn something practical with steel or wood,
Or maybe leather? Come, it's not too damp here.
You can stay dry and warm, we'll make our camp here.

DAR: You've been a good friend to me, true and strong.
In other circumstances —

DION: Don't go on.
We neither of us wanted what they planned.

DAR: No one should have their whole life pre-ordained.
Arranging marriage for two adolescents?
No. That's a path to sorrow and resentment.
To have a partner forced on you for life:
"You lucky kid, we've chosen you a wife"
— Or husband, spouse, or consort, or whatever —
Without a chance to look around?

DION: Ugh. Never!

DAR: It's like they're saying everything you do
From now on happens in a world of two.

DION: "We choose Prince Dion for you. Wed him promptly!"

DAR: "Here's Princess Dar. That's that. Your fate's accompli."
Forget exploring any other mate
Or anything at all. Just go stagnate.
Your story winds up here. End of the line.
One stupid face to look at for all time.

DION: There's no need to be hurtful —

DAR: Erp, I mean
Forget investigating other scenes.
Or for that matter, having your own story —
'Cause, truth to tell, I'm equally as boring.
I've never done a thing outside of school
But riding horses, playing music —

DION: Cool!

DAR: Or learning languages or playing polo,
Or blowing glass, composing for the oboe,
Or how to shoot a partridge at ten meters
And hand it over to the chef to feed us.

DION: You talk like that's all nothing. It's a lot!

DAR: But when it comes to real life, I've done squat.
Sure, I can hunt, fish, dance, and paint with oils,
And all the other tedious stuff that royals
May do to fill their time, but it's so dreary.
I want some friction in my life, you hear me?
A chance to make it on my own!

DION: I get it.

DAR: Or someday I'll be thirty and regret it.
I'm sure you're nice. You're fine. And if we had to,
Like if the world were ending, I'd be glad to —
Or if the human race was near to dying —

DION: We've pretty well established you're not buying.
Here, use my jacket if the ground's too hard.
A nice long sleep will help us be prepared
For where our quest may lead us —

DAR: No! I'm scared.
Let's just go back and tell them yes, we'll do it.
The truth is, we'd be wiser to go through it.

We could get eaten by a bear or panther.
Those birds sound nasty! Here's my final answer:
I'll marry you like everyone's expecting.
Why did we even think about objecting?
And hey, you're right, there's gonna be a storm.
Let's hurry home where we'll be dry and warm.
And later in the week—what were we dreading?
We'll join our kingdoms, and ourselves, by wedding!

DION: Your Majesty, we're both too good for settling.
You're tired and you're anxious. It's upsetting
To think there might be danger come to pass,
But for my money, you can kick the ass
Of any scary beast or weather system.
If nothing else, you'll *talk* 'em to submission.

DAR: Yes. Thanks for that. Right.

DION: No more second guessing.
No peddling backward, swerving, or regressing.
Tomorrow finds us swinging for the bleachers.
So no more talk of made-up scary creatures.
Just lie down. Go on. Close your eyes. Good night.

DAR: *(Yawning:)* That does sound good. You know, I think I might.
Hey, buddy? How's about a back-up scheme?
Let's meet here in a year if we're— *(Sleeps.)*

DION: Sweet dreams.

(Sound of rain.)

(Dion glances around, watchfully, then sleeps.)

(Erdos emerges.)

ERDOS: Two, yes, it's double,
But not much to say.

The options are polar,
It's towards or away.

It's northbound or southward,
Come here or get out.
Not complex or subtle:
A *whisper*, a SHOUT.

With two you know either
It's hell or it's heaven.
No real complications
Like five, say, or seven.

With two there's no issue,
No narrative drive.
There's not much to work with
Like seven or five.

Or three! Even three!

(Lights change; rain fades out.)

Three is win, place, or show.
With three, you get drama;
It's ready, set—

CORNELIUS: *(Entering a bakery:)* YO!

CONSTANCE: *(Entering. This scene takes place in the same location, but at a different time than Cornelius's scene:)* Helloooo?

CORNELIUS: You there? I need—

CONSTANCE: Excuse me? I'd like to buy something?

CORNELIUS: Yeah, hello! For my sister, please. Before she wakes up. I'm going to need one of the blueberry tarts. It's perfect for her. The color. That glossy purpley blue black. If she were a color, she'd be—

CONSTANCE: I was thinking a lemon bar? Or—? Sorry? Hello? It's our anniversary, the thing is. A sad day, but still—

CORNELIUS: I want to surprise her! Before she wakes up! She'll never believe I got up before her. I'll put it on her nightstand. "What's this?"

CONSTANCE: Worth celebrating. Not because it's sad. Because it's—

CORNELIUS: Us. Anniversary of us.

CONSTANCE: Or—when the bird died?

CORNELIUS: When our parents left—they were always leaving, but the *last* time they left, which we could tell was the last time. Mother packed all her nicest scarves, and the very last thing that happened was—

CONSTANCE: On their way out the door—

CORNELIUS: She said,

CONSTANCE: She said to him, to Father: "Bertram, your coat. Your good winter coat."

CORNELIUS: And it was *April.* And she looked at him significantly.

CONSTANCE: Like this?

(Constance and Cornelius both give a look.)

CORNELIUS: So we knew.

CONSTANCE: We knew.

CORNELIUS: And two days went by. We stared at each other, primarily. For two days. And then the canary—

CONSTANCE: Madame Vermicelli—

CORNELIUS: She was called something—it's slipped my—funny—

CONSTANCE: fell—

CORNELIUS: Madame Vermicelli, that was it—

CONSTANCE: she fell off her perch.

CORNELIUS: Dead.

CONSTANCE: We hadn't thought to feed her. We hadn't thought to feed *ourselves.*

CORNELIUS: And Constance said—

CONSTANCE: *(Calmly:)* "I see." And Cornelius burst into tears. Tears spurting out of his little face. "Cornelius," I said, "collect yourself."

CORNELIUS: She never scolded me! Never! She was the oldest, yes.

CONSTANCE: I'm older by ten months, but I try not to—

CORNELIUS: *I* was the one who—if anything—

CONSTANCE: Corey has always been the bold one.

CORNELIUS: Except this particular day. "Cornelius," she said, "collect yourself." She saved us.

CONSTANCE: "We're our own bird now, and our own parents, too. Bertram and Lydia are gone, and we're a family."

CORNELIUS: "No one can know. We can't have anyone splitting us up. So no telling anybody, ever." Oops.

CONSTANCE: Hello?

CORNELIUS: Well, I guess it doesn't matter anymore. We're old enough to—hey! I need a tart, you see. Blueberry. *That* one. The biggest.

CONSTANCE: Hello!

(Enter TREY.)

TREY: Yes?

CONSTANCE AND CORNELIUS: *(Each pointing:)* How much for that?

TREY: Uh, I don't really work here. I mean, I just clean up.

CORNELIUS: Well, where is somebody who can sell me a tart? And quickly, please. I want to surprise her.

TREY: They're all busy with the —

CONSTANCE: The wedding! Of course! I understand.

CORNELIUS: I don't understand. Is the shop open or not? Are these baked goods for sale, or not?

TREY: I guess you can have it.

CORNELIUS: Thank you so much!

TREY: That's a good story. Your brother. Your sister. The bird.

CONSTANCE: Cornelius.

CORNELIUS: Constance. Home.

(Trey hands something to Cornelius, who rewards him with a dazzling smile and exits. Trey stares after him, smitten.)

CONSTANCE: How much?

TREY: Uh...five?

CONSTANCE: That seems very fair. Here you go.

(Constance pays and exits; Trey remains for a moment, taken with her. Exits.)

(Rain. Dawn. Dion and Dar on the ground, Erdos nearby. Dion stirs.)

DION: *(Quiet alarm:)* I slept too long. The sun is sneaking through.
By now I should have been long gone from you.
The world is round, or so they say, my dear.
If it is meant to be, I'll meet you here
In twenty days and nights, or twenty thousand,
When we our futures and our depths have sounded.

(Dion picks up his pack and backs away from Dar, crouching. He smacks into Erdos.)

I beg your pardon! How much did you hear?

ERDOS: Not much. Some gooey stuff. Oh, and "my dear."

DION: Can you be cool?

ERDOS: My lips are sealed, I swear.
But you don't seem to want to leave her there.

DION: It's complicated, that's all I can say.

ERDOS: It always is. That's why I stay away
From all that stuff and focus on mathematics.
No complications, romance, or dramatics.

DION: You mean to tell me you're some kind of hermit?

ERDOS: Not some kind, but *exactly*. I confirm it.
I like it here. It's quiet. I can focus.
And no one bothers me! No noise or ruckus.
My days I spend in happy contemplation
Of numbers—add, subtract, multiplication.
And after that I often observe others
Like vagabonds or pickpockets or lovers
Who've found it best to sneak away by night.

DION: You do this voluntarily?

ERDOS: That's right.

DION: But isn't there a family to miss you?
A mom to hug you? Sibling slug or kiss you?
A family of three or five or seven?
You must have someone—

ERDOS: Youngest of eleven.

(Dar stirs in her sleep, mutters.)

DAR: Purn durfer?

DION: I should be off. Quick! Your story!

ERDOS: Then may I speak in prose?

DION: Of course, go for it.

ERDOS: I was left on the roof of a coach as a baby. Nobody saw me fall off except my next closest sister. I bounced down the road in my baby seat, and all she did was blow raspberries at me through the back window. Plllllph! Fortunately, I wasn't hurt, and soon I was taken in by a poor but honest flock of mathematicians and number theorists who were happy to have an extra set of fingers and toes around. They fed me on donuts and bagels from the break room. When I turned sixteen, they handed me a bundt cake and told me it was time to go make my own way in the world. And would I mind if they just grabbed a slice and ate at their desks, because they did need to be getting back to it, so good luck then, and off you go!

And here I am.

DION: A hermit. And why not if that's your thing?

ERDOS: But what of you, sir?

DION: Sir?

ERDOS: Your dad's the King?

DION: I guess I'm not the greatest at disguise.

ERDOS: A little dirt might help to fool the eyes.

(Dion begins to smear dirt on himself.)

DION: Say, you won't tell?

ERDOS: Tell who? This valley's empty!

DION: There's surely a reward.

ERDOS: That doesn't tempt me.

DION: I'll need some work.

ERDOS: The village may have openings.

DION: The village! Right. I'll do my best.

ERDOS: Here's hoping.
Good day then, sir! I mean, good day, uh, *you.*

(Exits.)

DION: Good day. And to you, Princess Dar, adieu.

(Lights up on Cornelius up a tree, writing in a journal; Constance on a bench, working with papers. As before, they are in separate times and spaces.)

(Trey enters between them, raking leaves. He starts to read over Constance's shoulder.)

TREY: Volunt.

CONSTANCE: What?

TREY: *Volunt.* Isn't it? "We want." Not *volent.* "We will want." Oh hey, it's you. Lemon bar.

CONSTANCE: My brother is. I bought it. I mean yes. I mean Hi.

CORNELIUS: Hi.

TREY: *(To Cornelius:)* I like your shoes. *(To Constance:)* Volo. "Wishing, wanting."

CORNELIUS: Thank you.

TREY: *(To Cornelius:)* You're up my tree, actually.

CORNELIUS: What?

TREY: That's my tree. For sitting. No problem now, but when I take a break...

CORNELIUS: *(Starting to flirt:)* I don't think it's your tree.

TREY: Of course. Trees belong to everyone. To mother earth. But that is my branch.

CONSTANCE: You know a lot of Latin for a — baker? Leaf raker?

TREY: You know surprisingly little Latin for a — ?

CONSTANCE: Tutor. For the royal nieces and nephews.

TREY: Really? *(To Cornelius:)* Move over.

CORNELIUS: There's not room for two of us.

TREY: Move over so you can see. On the branch. Behind your left knee, it says "Octavia plus Sisto."

CORNELIUS: *(Looks.)* Nope.

TREY: *(To Constance:)* Must be nutsy at the palace. What with the couple run off and all.

CONSTANCE: Nutsy is exactly what it is.

TREY: How are those little nephews and nieces? Bit of a handful? *(To Cornelius:)* Double or nothing?

CORNELIUS: Double what?

TREY: *(Covering his eyes:)* Under your right hand it says

"Norman sucks dill pickles."

CORNELIUS: *(Looking:)* Nope. Though that might be a *drawing* of a dill pickle.

TREY: Why are you in a tree?

CORNELIUS: Why not?

TREY: Call it a hunch, but I don't think when you got dressed this morning, your plan was to sit in a tree.

CORNELIUS: I'm hiding. I work at the palace. It's a nutsy day. What with the royal couple run off.

TREY: What do you do?

CORNELIUS: Assistant Stylist. If the wedding ever happens, and if you ever get to see the bridesmaids' dresses —

TREY: — unlikely —

CORNELIUS: — the petticoats were my idea.

TREY: You must be so proud.

CORNELIUS: Shut up.

CONSTANCE: Oh, they're darling!

TREY: What's that?

CONSTANCE: My students?

TREY: I shouldn't have interrupted your work.

CONSTANCE: I'm glad you did. Whoo! I'm trying to be bolder. Like my brother.

TREY: The lemon bar. Did he like it?

CONSTANCE: Four bites.

TREY: Chomp. Chomp. Chomp. Chomp. That is bold.

CONSTANCE: He left me one.

TREY: Chomp.

CONSTANCE: We share everything.

TREY: No, really. Petticoats! Fantastic.

CORNELIUS: I suppose you save little orphaned puppies in your spare—hey! What *do* you do? I thought you worked at the bakery.

TREY: I do.

CORNELIUS: Are you lost?

TREY: I do a little bit of everything. I'm a factotum.

CORNELIUS: Is that a fact?

TREY: *(Climbing up to get closer:)* Totally.

CONSTANCE: You have to be. Bold. These days.

TREY: These days? How old are you?

CONSTANCE: I'm old-fashioned, I guess. Not on purpose.

TREY: No, it's nice.

CORNELIUS: For whom?

TREY: Hmm?

CORNELIUS: For whom do you factotum?

TREY: Factote. The verb is factote.

CONSTANCE: I mean, if I were my brother right now, I'd have done something bold.

(Cornelius and Trey are almost kissing.)

TREY: Like what?

CONSTANCE: Like—

CORNELIUS: Here! *(Writing on Trey's hand:)* Here's my name and the color of my house. If you can find me, we'll have a picnic.

CONSTANCE: Like invite you on a picnic. Tell you where we live.

(Trey pulls his sleeve down over his hand.)

TREY: *(To Constance:)* I'd love to see you again.

CONSTANCE: Me too!

TREY: Early mornings, I'm at the bakery. I'll take a break if you come by.

CONSTANCE: What time?

TREY: Anytime.

CORNELIUS: I should get down. Out of this tree.

CONSTANCE: I should get back to work.

TREY: Good luck with the royal people.

CONSTANCE AND CORNELIUS: Thanks.

CONSTANCE: Will you tell me your name?

CORNELIUS: Aren't you going to tell me your name?

TREY: Trey.

CONSTANCE AND CORNELIUS: Trey.

(They all see each other and register what's happening. Disbelieving, they move into a triangle. Trey, in a mild panic, extends his arms to keep them all at a safe distance.)

(Lights.)

DAR: *(Rising:)* This isn't good. That ground was awfully wet. My trousers feel like diapers. You can bet

He woke up early, headed someplace dry.
"Oh, look! Let's camp here!" Sure, why not, let's try.
"And by the way, I'll slip out in the a.m.,
And leave you to the bugs and beasts and mayhem."
(Unrolling Dion's jacket and putting it on:) I miss him though.
No, no, I don't miss *him.*
Just—what? His voice, his eyes, his hands, his grin.
Oh, hell. I'm sure it's just because I'm lonely.
No. Step it up. Today my job is only
To look for food, and work, and some good lodging,
And then there's always bloodhounds to be dodging.
Forget him! Up and at it, that's the plan.
And not another thought about that man.

> *(Dar exits.)*

> *(Light change. Constance, Cornelius, and Trey are still in place.)*

> *(From another direction, QUERY enters, an odd little sneaky person carrying a parchment flyer with the word "REWARD" large and visible. Query circles Constance, Cornelius, and Trey at a distance, comparing them to the flyer in her hand. They are too busy to notice. When Query has examined them thoroughly, she exits.)*

TREY: It's no one's fault.

CORNELIUS: Obviously. I mean, if it *were* anyone's fault...

CONSTANCE: It's not. I won't do anything that would hurt my brother.

CORNELIUS: Really? I'm the one who's going to get hurt?

CONSTANCE: Corey?

CORNELIUS: Constance? *(To Trey:)* Are you planning to juggle us?

TREY: No. No! I was involved with *one* person once, and I couldn't even keep *that* in the air.

CORNELIUS: Fine. But now what?

TREY: I have a proposal. If we don't see each other, nothing bad will happen. I'm not saying I like this—

CONSTANCE: It does seem like the best way.

TREY: So. I stay away from the palace and the upper grounds. And you avoid the bakery and the park. Anywhere else we might run into each other?

CONSTANCE: I hate to claim the library, but...the library. I spend most of my weekends there. Corey?

CORNELIUS: The dance club. The art galleries. The zoo.

CONSTANCE: I'm afraid we're taking over everything.

TREY: That's all right. I'll spend more time practicing guitar.

CONSTANCE AND CORNELIUS: You play guitar?

CORNELIUS: No, no. Sober up.

(Puts out a hand to shake Trey's, solemnly.)

Goodbye.

TREY: Goodbye.

CONSTANCE: *(Shaking hands:)* Goodbye.

TREY: Goodbye. *(Starts to exit.)* Write me! Just kidding.

(Exits.)

CORNELIUS: Well done. Proud of us.

CONSTANCE: Yes.

CORNELIUS: Are you disappointed though?

CONSTANCE: Are you?

CORNELIUS: No. I mean, a little. I liked him. But you're the one who's...

CONSTANCE: What? Oh. Say it.

CORNELIUS: You're the one who's never had a boyfriend.

CONSTANCE: I haven't needed one. I don't need one.

CORNELIUS: I couldn't bear to lose you.

CONSTANCE: You never will.

CORNELIUS: All right. *(Beat.)* Any word on the royal runaways?

CONSTANCE: I guess we'll all hear if anything happens. And the little lords and ladies still need their lessons. Walk with me?

CORNELIUS: At least you have something to do. Only so many times you can iron a bridesmaid dress. Boring.

CONSTANCE: Make yourself a fancy hat from scraps.

CORNELIUS: I'll make *you* a fancy hat.

CONSTANCE: *(Kissing Cornelius on the forehead:)* You're a fancy hat.

(They exit.)

(Erdos enters, counting his steps under his breath. Dar enters, sees him, tries to catch up.)

DAR: Excuse me. Sorry! Hi? Hello? YOU HEAR ME?

ERDOS: Eleven, thirteen...maybe not so near me?
I'm trying to work out a complex pattern
Not to be rude, but there's no time for chatter.

DAR: I'll leave you if you'll help me find some food,

Or point me toward some work, however crude.
It's been a while since I ate or drank,
I cannot pay you, but you'd have my thanks.
If you'll give me a hand, I swear I'll vanish.
The thing is, I'm persistent when I'm famished.

ERDOS: That jacket's nice. I'll take it for some porridge.

DAR: Oh no, it's not for sale.

ERDOS: You'd rather forage?

DAR: It's just that...

ERDOS: Someone special left it with you?

DAR: What? No! I'm catching cold! I need it! *(Sneezing:)*
CHOO!
Now, what about a job? Will you not help me?
I'm smart, I'm—uh, I'm game, I'm fairly healthy.
I'm smashing at a dance, a real go-getter!
There must be someone hiring minuetters?
Or how about glass-blowing? 'Cause I'm aces
At turning fire and sand to jugs and vases.
Or then again, if what you need's translation,
I know them all, from Farsi to Dalmatian.

ERDOS: Your Highness, if you really don't mind labor—

DAR: My *Highness*? No! I'm just a woodsy neighbor,
Just out to gather kindling before night,
And looking for some poor provisions.

ERDOS: Right.
Don't worry, I don't care, won't tell, won't ask.
Though I would think you'd maybe wear a mask?
But anyway, if work is what you seek,
You might look at the inn across the creek.
I've also heard the pub will pay in scraps

For someone to clean out the oil traps.

DAR: My hero! It's experience I crave.

ERDOS: And off you go.

DAR: I'll leave you to your...cave?

(Dar exits; Erdos retires.)

(Trey enters with a pair of garden clippers. He starts tending to a tree or bush.)

(Constance re-enters with a book.)

CONSTANCE: Oh! No, no. Wrong way.

TREY: Turned around?

CONSTANCE: I have a terrible sense of direction.

TREY: Me too!

(They share a brief swoon.)

NO! Exactly what we're not doing. Right?

CONSTANCE: Right!

TREY: *(Crossing past her:)* Goodbye! *(As he nears the exit:)* Oh.

CONSTANCE: What's that?

TREY: Nothing.

CONSTANCE: I thought you said "oh."

TREY: Couple of turtles, that's all.

CONSTANCE: Turtles?

TREY: Kind of old. Couple of eighty-year-old turtles. Looks like he's waiting for her to get ready. You know, like an old married couple.

CONSTANCE: Really? *(Runs over to see.)* Awww.

TREY: "Come on, Myrtle, the opera starts at eight."

CONSTANCE: "Keep your pants on, Blurtle, just trying to make myself pretty for you."

TREY: "You're *always* pr—" No. Right. Gotta go.

CONSTANCE: I'll see you. I won't.

TREY: Check check. Bye.

CONSTANCE: Bye.

> (*Trey exits. Cornelius enters, carrying snowshoes, which he then tries awkwardly to put on.*)

> (*Trey re-enters with a snow shovel, sees Cornelius from the back.*)

TREY: How great is this snow! (*As Cornelius turns:*) It's you. I'll go.

CORNELIUS: Do you mind? It's just—winter! I love winter.

TREY: Me too! (*A moment.*) Who cares? So do lots of people. (*Exiting:*) Hey!

CORNELIUS: Something?

TREY: Nope. Not at all.

CORNELIUS: Great.

TREY: Just a couple of puppies.

CORNELIUS: Good for them.

TREY: Trying to get up on their feet. Looks like the first time.

CORNELIUS: Stupid.

TREY: I know. (*Beat.*) You have to come see this right now!

> (*Cornelius runs over. They watch puppies.*)

CORNELIUS: Do you think they're warm enough?

TREY: Not at all!

CORNELIUS: Send warm thoughts.

TREY: Hot cocoa.

CORNELIUS: Thick sweaters, you guys. Brrrr. MMMM.

TREY: Cuddling under big warm blankets. Nope.

CORNELIUS: Damn. Well, I guess —

TREY: No, totally.

CORNELIUS: I mean, watching puppies together.

(Gestures as if to say "how goofy is that?")

TREY: Yeah. Why do animals insist on doing cute things around us?

CORNELIUS: No *us*.

TREY: Exactly. Bye.

CORNELIUS: Bye.

(Cornelius exits.)

(Sound of wind, loud.)

(Trey runs into Constance, head down, heading into the wind, carrying some cloth bags.)

TREY: Whoops!

CONSTANCE: Whoops!

TREY: Shopping?

CONSTANCE: I don't like seeing you.

TREY: I'm sorry.

(Heads the other way, runs into Cornelius.)

CORNELIUS: *(Walking, clutched against the wind, head down:)* Ugh, the snow is so dirty now. *(Sees Trey.)* Quit it!

TREY: I'm not trying to—

CORNELIUS: Well you're doing a bad job of it.

(Trey changes direction, now face-to-face with Constance.)

CONSTANCE: If you run into Cornelius?

TREY: I won't.

CONSTANCE: If you accidentally do—he would like that turtle thing I think.

(Trey turns in place.)

CORNELIUS: If anything, you should be with my sister. Show her those puppies.

(Constance and Cornelius see each other.)

CONSTANCE: Oh no!

CORNELIUS: I'll go.

TREY: This

CONSTANCE: Has

CORNELIUS: Got

TREY: To

CONSTANCE: Stop.

CORNELIUS: Agreed.

TREY: I say we take a leaf from the royals. I'll head out of town. Start fresh. I don't mind. Nobody will miss me here. Except, obviously, you two.

CONSTANCE: Be well!

CORNELIUS: Take care!

(They head off, Trey separate from the others, but Constance and Cornelius soon drift apart and each of them drifts closer to Trey, till they are traveling in a big triangle around the stage, trying to stay safely away from each other.)

(Query sneaks in and begins to stalk them. She follows each one for a moment, comparing them to the flyer she holds.)

(Trey turns suddenly; Query speeds away.)

TREY: Weird. Anyway, *(Stopping:)* this ought to do it. *(Sees Constance and Cornelius.)* Damn.

CORNELIUS: Hey!

CONSTANCE: Oh, come on!

TREY: You! North! You! West! Me! This way!

(Erdos peeps out of his cave, glaring.)

(The trio exits, meets again.)

You! To the sea! You! To the icecaps! Me! To the high volcanoes!

(They exit. Erdos waits. They meet again.)

(Erdos lurches out and growls.)

ERDOS: To Mars! To Venus! To Saturn!

CORNELIUS: Do you mind?

TREY: We're trying not to do something.

CONSTANCE: But it isn't working.

CORNELIUS: You know what? We're all terrible at directions. Maybe we should *try* to meet here.

(A beat while they take this in.)

TREY: That should do it.

CONSTANCE: Sure. So this is it then. Really goodbye.

ERDOS: Oh, yes, by all means. Just not on my doorstep. Is that a remote possibility?

CONSTANCE: Sorry.

TREY: Our bad.

CORNELIUS: Off we go.

(Constance and Cornelius exit together; Trey separately.)

ERDOS: Three. How exhausting.
No thank you. Please stop.
So flipping unstable.
Slip, wobble, kerplop.

Now *four*, that's more like it.
No drama, no clatter.
With four you learn quickly
There's nothing the matter.

(He beings arranging four of something on the ground — maybe rocks and pinecones, or his shoes and socks.)

Four moves two by two,
Like Noah's collection.
It's easy to simplify,
Just a bisection.

(Moving the objects into pairs in different combinations:) It's easy to break up,
Cinchy to split;
A couple of twos
Are the pieces of it.

(Growing bored:) As a matter of fact,
It's a big waste of time

Considering numbers
Other than prime.

What I like are those numbers
That stand by themselves
That can't be divided
By anything else.

Four's not worth the wind-up,
So let me be frank
And say like a Frenchman:
Un deux trois quatre cinq.

Or even in German,
That "funf" looks like fun,
The countdown's beginning:
Five four three two —

QUINN: *(Off:)* RUN!

(Erdos is nearly run over as QUINN, QUEENIE, QUENTIN, QUEESY, and QUERY enter and begin to dance, a raucous hybrid of Scottish fling and punk.)

(They end with a flourish.)

(Erdos backs to the edge of the stage.)

Tonight will be epic, I feel!

QUENTIN: The ground here's just right for a reel!

QUEASY: My legs are on fire,
And I'm mad with desire:
Hold me down or I'll start to cartwheel!

QUENTIN: Wait! Something does not feel okay here.

QUEASY: But you reconnoitered all day here!

QUENTIN: I smell something odd.

I think—oh my god!
(Turns on Erdos.) A little rat's joined us to play here.

(They advance on Erdos, quickly surrounding him so he has no way to exit.)

QUINN: You're way out of line. You were silly
To spy on us for our dad. Really.
You need to get lost,
If you don't, there's a cost.
Our Quentin will tear off your willy.

ERDOS: You've got it all wrong; you're mistaken.
I swear I'm not trying to break in.
Your shindig looks lively,
But I'm not a spy, see,
I'm just here for some calculations.

QUENTIN: This gathering's private, you creeper.

QUEASY: We love teaching lessons to peepers.

QUENTIN: We don't like your nerve;

QUEASY: We're not soft on pervs.

QUEENIE: *(Sneaking up behind Erdos, startling him:)* Say hi
when you meet the Grim Reaper!

ERDOS: Gah! Listen, I'm no Peeping Tom.
I won't tell your dad. Or your mom!
Though I look like I'm caught,
My intentions are naught
But observing. Let's all just stay calm.

QUINN: At least you've got one thing to boast—
You've made it much farther than most.
Too bad it's for nada,
You trespassed. We gotta
Enforce our restrictions. You're toast.

ERDOS: I mean you no harm! Really, none!
I'm making a study. From One
To Infinity...ish
It's long been my wish —
Right now, though, I wish I could *run*!

(*A moment of tense silence, then Quinn breaks into a big smile.*)

QUINN: Ah, screw it, you don't seem half bad.
We've nothing against you, my lad.
You seem pretty mellow,
A nice little fellow.

QUEASY: And what's more, you'd look good in plaid.

(*Roars of approval from the Qs, who begin wrapping Erdos in scarves, etc., as he speaks.*)

ERDOS: You mean it? You're not gonna pound me?
You'll just dance and caper around me?
I'm so glad you get
That I'm no kind of threat!
In fact, now I'm happy you found me!

QUEASY: We're not gonna beat you, that's true,
But now here's what we're gonna do:
We won't dance without you;
This party's *about* you!
You're part of the gang now.

ALL Qs: WOO HOO!

QUENTIN: Get up now, get jiggy, get on it.
And dance like there's bees in your bonnet.
We don't have all night,
Get dancing, that's right.
It's easy, you'll see when you've done it.

(Dancing, in which Erdos is passed from partner to partner. Finally he steps out, winded, bent over double and holding his side.)

ERDOS: My god! They're relentless. No pity.
I'm worn out and nauseous and giddy.

QUINN: Hey!

QUENTIN: Where's—?

QUEASY: You get hopping!
We're nowhere near stopping!

ERDOS: I think I would rather they hit me
(As the Qs approach, to distract them:) Hey, guys, can I ask you to say
How you manage these late-night soirèes?
Your parents don't catch you?
Does nobody watch you?
How do you have such time to play?

QUINN: We've worked out a scheme that's real shrewd:
There's no tracking such a big brood.
With five, you can always
Sneak one down a hallway,
And they size things up unpursued.

(As Query pantomimes this:) Our Query's the sneakiest sneak;
She flies down the hall for a peek,
And when things are hushed,
She comes back all flushed,
And gives us the thumbs-up we seek.

QUEENIE: Once she signals, we slip and we creep,
While the parents are counting their sheep.
Then we're back in by dawn
When we "wake" with a yawn

And pretend that we've been sound asleep.

Though lately they've been awfully curious
About one thing they find quite mysterious:
Our shoes wear out so
Which costs lots of dough.
If they really knew why, they'd be furious!

ERDOS: Wow! You've sure got it wired—

QUENTIN: You brat!
Distracting us with all this chat!
You got us to talking,
And sitting and gawking.
Let's dance now, and no more of that!

ERDOS: I don't think I can, I'm too—

QUEASY: Rubbish!
You're in your prime, don't be so sluggish.
It's time you get skipping,
And stomping and ripping,
And helping us raise tonight's rumpus!

QUINN: Once you start, you will find nothing's finer.
It's better than sex! It's diviner!
And with one extra—YOU—
We may see something new!

ERDOS: And that just may be my stomach liner.

Besides, I have much more to ask.
How can you be up to the task?
Sure, dancing's faboo,
But the way that you do—
So boisterous, so long, and so fast!

QUEASY: By daytime, we all toe the line.
Between school and our jobs, it's a grind.

Our spirits get sapped,
Our energy zapped,
Time to party or else lose your mind!

QUINN: The pressure all day is immense,
It's exhausting, the whole future tense.
"What's your plan?" "Which career?"
"Whatcha doing next year?"
Dancing hard is our only defense!

QUENTIN: No more interruptions, let's move!
Nothing else feels as good as a groove.
Your mama did bless you
With a backside, and yes, you
Better shake like you've something to prove.

> *(Enter Dion, unseen by the others. He wears an apron and carries a toolkit.)*

> *(Erdos gets thrown out of the dance on a wide spin and checks in with the audience, while the movement behind him winds down.)*

ERDOS: No kidding, I'm this close to herking.
It's too much for me, this berserking.
What's that? They've abated!
And before I'm belated!
Hoo-ee, I can breathe now. It's working.

QUINN: All right, that's an hour, let's check.
Our boots can't be worn out or wrecked.
They have to look good still,
As if we've just stood still.
How are they? Oh, crap.

QUENTIN: Ick.

QUEASY: Yuck.

QUEENIE: Bleck.

QUINN: Oh hell no! My shoes are in tatters.

QUENTIN: And mine are all shredded and shattered.

QUEASY: The stitching's in pieces,
There's sweat in the creases.

QUEENIE: They're nothing like new. That's what matters.

Our parents will lose it—no joke.
We'll all be locked up till we croak.
We'll spend our life grounded,
Barbed-wire-surrounded.
And every privilege revoked.

QUEASY: We can never again misbehave.
Which means that tonight's our last rave.
Will we turn it down?

ALL: Never!

QUEENIE: We'll dance harder than ever.

ERDOS: Then I'm cooked! There's no chance I'll be saved.

(The Qs turn on Erdos and dance him faster than before.)

DION: Hey! What is this hullabaloo?
I'm here with a newsflash for you!
If it's meant to be joyous,
I'm afraid that this boy is
In line for the hospital.

ALL: BOO!

DION: I suppose it's not really my business,
But you're pushing this guy to the limit.
If it's shoes that need tending,
I'm all set for mending.
Just sit down and give me a minute.

(The Qs look angry and suspicious.)

What's to lose? I can see that you're hobbling.
I'd be happy to offer my cobbling
To your whole entourage,
And throw in a massage.
Your poor worn-out feet must be throbbing.

(The Qs put their heads together, then break on a loud grunt.)

QUINN: Let's see what you got, little fixer.
For our rips and our tears and our blisters,
Our flopping-off soles,
And our straggly holes.
After that, we'll get back to our mixer.

(Dion gestures to them to line up. Erdos, limping and panting, crosses to behind Dion, where he can watch but be protected from the Qs.)

ERDOS: Thank god! You just saved me, my friend.
They were dancing my life to an end.
I'm aching and thirsty,
And my lungs are, well, bursty.
Their shoes and my *legs* need a mend!

(Erdos watches as Quentin, then Queasy, gets a mend and polish from Dion. The shoe repair process is quick and stylized: a tug, a twist, a shine.)

(Meanwhile, Queenie turns away and retouches her hair and makeup with the help of Query.)

DION: Never mind, it's my pleasure, good man.
I need practice, and this sweaty clan,
With their feet so disgusting,
Will need lots of adjusting.

ERDOS: Thanks a heap! Stall them long as you can.

(After Dion has spruced them up, Quentin and Queasy go into a little soft shoe to celebrate. Dion can't help himself and joins in, then increases the level of difficulty. He's got moves.)

(Then he hurries back to work on Queenie, who turns to face him just as he sits back down. They draw everyone's focus.)

QUEENIE: I swear, if you mess up my shoes —

DION: You can thrash me however you choose.
But first give me a try,
And you might find that I —

QUEENIE: Oh, that's nice. That's the stuff! Oh aah ooh.

(When they are finished, Queenie struts away.)

(Dion works on Query's shoes, while Queenie moves to Erdos, who is simultaneously terrified and wowed by her.)

Your friend's awful cute. What's his deal?
His hands did a job on my heels!
Do you think he's attracted?

ERDOS: He certainly acted —

QUEENIE: Introduce me, you fool! Now! For real!

ERDOS: I'd like you to meet —

QUEENIE: My name's Queenie!

ERDOS: May I introduce —

QUEENIE: You're so dreamy!
And is that by chance
An awl in your pants,
Or are you just happy to see me?

DION: Oh my gosh! You're a knock-out for sure,
And no doubt lots of guys would endure
Any hardship or trial.

The difference is I'll
Have to leave now, despite your allure.

QUEENIE: Do you not understand what I mean?
Look around. See these thugs? I'm their queen.
So you'll do what I say,
And you'll like it that way,
'Cause I don't kid around when I'm keen.

DION: But I'm already spoke for and promised.

QUEENIE: I don't give a sh—

ERDOS: Shh! I got this.
His secret? He's clutzy.
Tremendously!

QUEENIE: But—

ERDOS: See?

(Dion falls down to illustrate.)

He's got two left feet.

QUEENIE: Really?

DION: Honest!

QUEENIE: Then this all might as well be forgotten.
That's the one thing I simply can't cotton.
Let's throw in the towel,
And say no harm, no foul,
I just *can't*, if your dancing is rotten!

QUENTIN: *(Grabbing Dion:)* Hey, what was that step you just showed us?
You start to the left, *that* I noticed.
Then after the slide,
Is it step, ball, change, glide?
Or—step-step, hop-hop?

QUEENIE: Oh, you're bogus!

(Queenie moves into a stand-off with Dion. He's busted. He starts to pack up. Meanwhile, the other Qs surround Queenie sympathetically.)

Hell, I don't know what I was thinking.
The guys that I like — always stinking.
Whether chewing tobaccky,
Or smoking the wacky.
The one before this? Too much drinking.

And this pattern's so bloody recurrent.
Is it me? Are my looks the deterrent?
I get all of the losers,
The louses, the boozers.
How I hate it and wish that they weren't!

(Erdos girds himself up and approaches Queenie.)

ERDOS: If I may? It just can't be that bleak.
There are so many fish in the creek.
And by "fish," I mean *guys* who
Would give their right eyes to
Be near you for even a week.

QUEENIE: No, don't patronize me, you crumb.
You can save your clichés. I'm not dumb.
Yeah, your friend is a hunk,
But I'm done with that junk.
I just want to dance till I'm numb.

(Erdos retreats, mortified. Queenie dances.)

(Dar enters, in janitor's coveralls, hair in a kerchief, wearing Dion's jacket. Dion spots Dar and switches gears abruptly.)

DION: Yes, dance. But with me. Let's get festive!
Please teach me your moves. They're impressive.

QUEENIE: What? That's quite a change.

DION: I know it seems strange,
But my legs are quite suddenly restive.

(Dar watches them dance for a second, then stomps up and gets in Dion's face. Dion keeps dancing.)

Why, what is this! I didn't see you there.

DAR: You didn't see me, or just didn't care?

DION: I know this can't be jealousy I see.
You never had the slightest use for me.

DAR: Of course not! I was in the neighborhood
And thought I'd let you know that all is good.

DION: Me, too! It turns out I've a gift for shoes.
I'll start a business, once I've paid my dues.
It was so smart to take that daring plunge
And find ourselves. So glad we played that hunch.

DAR: And me, my new life's better than I hoped.
I work three jobs and *love* the smell of soap.
And finding somewhere warm to sleep is easy
When I get off my last shift cleaning feces
And washing floors where urine has grown crusty.
It takes a lot more than that to disgust me.
You were so scared before! So doom-and-gloomy.
My god, it's lucky that you listened to me.

DION: I'm glad you're happy, though in truth I'd claim
Your memories and mine are not the same.
As I remember,

QUEENIE: *(Interrupting:)*   What is this, you cur!
You're up to something—what's the deal with her?

DION: I'm sorry if I gave the wrong impression.

QUEENIE: Don't give me that. I just asked you a question.

You told me your heart was bespoken,
And mine was about to be broken,
Till this person arrived,
Then you hopped up and jived,
Was it all just an act? Were you joking?

DAR: Is that right? Was it all just a trick?

QUEENIE: To make this one jealous?

DAR: That's sick.

QUEENIE: You embarrass and shame me,
And no one could blame me
If I beat your face with a stick.

DAR: Don't touch him!

QUEENIE: Try and stop me.

DION: *(To Dar:)*   Do you care?

DAR: Of course not. Couldn't matter less, I swear.

DION: That's good because our lives are separate.

DAR: Exactly. Is there something you don't get?

DION: Nope. See you. Glad to hear it's going fine.

DAR: *(Turning back:)* I guess one question does come to my mind.
You told that dishy redhead you're engaged,
Around the time she went and got enraged.
(Raising her voice:) That's right! You said "your heart was not your own."
Congratulations! Anyone I know?

DION: You're flattering yourself if you think that.

Nice jacket, by the way.

DAR: Here, take it back!

ERDOS: Oh no. Not three!
Another triangle? Can't be.

CORNELIUS: *(Entering:)* Then again, you might get used to it.
(Seeing Constance:) Ah! There you are.

CONSTANCE: *(Entering:)* One hundred eighty degrees equals
misery. Or does it?

TREY: *(Entering:)* It seemed a given: that way madness lies.

CONSTANCE: But there's a nice familiar ache to triangles.

CORNELIUS: A stable instability.

TREY: Equilaterally distributed.

DION: No triangles! Don't pay them any mind.
I'm sorry, Queenie. I was out of line.
Believe me, I never —

QUEENIE: Don't even. Whatever.
You can dig your own grave. I'll be fine.

*(Quentin and Query have been circling Dion and Dar. When
Queenie turns toward them, they signal wildly, which she
misunderstands.)*

What now? Oh it's dawn? Great, we're stuck now.
Can't go forward or back, that's our luck now.

QUENTIN: Look, Queenie — these two!

QUEENIE: Give it up, guys, please do.

QUEASY: It's the couple!

QUEENIE: I don't give a — *what* now?

QUINN: Although you've been somewhat debased.

This time wasn't truly a waste,
If my eyes aren't liars,
They're the two on the flyer.
The very same pair that we've chased!

QUENTIN: It's our gambit for getting home late!
We'll be heroes, not hoodlums. It's great.
We just turn these two over,
Collect all the silver,
And buy ourselves all the—

DAR: No, wait!
You cannot think it fair to turn us in.
To make us marry without love's a sin.
(To Dion:) And you don't love me, right? Not even any?

DION: Do *you* love *me?*

DAR: Of course not. Don't be funny.
(To the Qs:) You see, it would be quite despicable
To force us to live lives so miserable.

QUEENIE: We couldn't give a damn. Rules of the hunt.

DAR: Don't anger your new King and Queen up front.
If you don't give a fig for common virtue,
Come back with us and pay for breaking curfew.

DION: Although we'll face some shame on our return,
We'll see you get the punishment you've earned.

(The Qs are confounded. Everyone is at an impasse.)

ERDOS: My head. My brain.
Such friction. Such pain.
Such fractiousness among so few.
And that's just five and three and two.

DAR: So now hear this. The valley we'll divide
And tolerate each other, side by side.

(Dion directs them around; they start to move into separate quadrants, The Qs, the trio, and Dion separate from Dar.)

(Enter ALFA, BERNIE, CHARLEY, DELTA, ERNIE, FARLEY, and GREG. They look scruffy and neglected, with tattered clothes, makeshift backpacks, a couple of walking sticks they've picked up along the way.)

ALFA: What's up? We come in peace.

BERNIE: In pieces, too.

CHARLEY: We mean you no harm.

DELTA: We're unarmed.

ERNIE: Just need a place to land is all.

FARLEY: Just need a hand.

QUINN: You need to go back where you're from.
This valley is all out of room.
So go! Head on back,
Just retrace your tracks.
We've nothing to offer. Go home.

(The seven new people stand paralyzed.)

QUENTIN: Hey! Did you not hear what we said?
Back home with you, that's where you head.

ALFA: That's one thing we can't do.
Be merciful, can't you?
The country we're from wants us dead.

(A sudden shift in mood. Everyone senses that the stakes are real.)

DION: The way you speak, it has a certain weight.
We will at least hear why you've drawn this fate.

CONSTANCE: No matter what though,

CORNELIUS: They must depart this place.

TREY: That's for freakin' sure.

DAR: For now, go ahead, let us hear.
Though you can't stay, there's nothing to fear.

BERNIE: Tell 'em, Alf.

ALFA: Older parents, had their struggles. Loved each other, but no fruit. Went to a healer, she's for real, gives them a potion, says "Here's my bill."
Doctor comes, says "here's your bundle, give it a cuddle. Oh! here's another. You're a mother two times. No wait, I'm not done, here you got another one—hope you like some girls too." Ma says, "Doctor, yeah, I do!"
Doc says "congrats then, here's a few more brats then." Dad says "please don't call 'em that. All we've waited, hoping praying, glad to have them all."
Doc says, "Better call a baby sitter, mister, 'cause you got a litter! Should have thinned the herd some."
Dad says, "You get out, you're done."
Ma says "Bless them, every one."
Doc says "Hey, before I go? Glad that you're so glad to claim them, and here's my bill. Don't forget to name them!"

BERNIE: Daddy's scared now, seeing he's the breadwinner. How's he gonna pay off all these creditors? Feed nine people, that's tough, too. Better take a few more jobs, always more to do. Won't see the critters much but make it through.

CHARLEY: Ma says "I don't care what it cost us. I love each one of them." And here's the roster:

ALFA: Alfa

BERNIE: Bernie

CHARLEY: Charley

DELTA: Delta

ERNIE: Ernie

FARLEY: Farley

GREG: *(A beat late:)* Hmm? Oh. Greg.

ALFA: Growing up septuplets, wouldn't give it up,
Wouldn't trade it, even when that made it hard.
We were really close, see,
Coming from the same womb,
Same there in the nursery room,
Wrapped up and huggy,
Made our parents buggy.
Took a minute sometimes, waiting to get fed;
Competing for resources of course isn't always happy.
Sometimes you got to wait for a fresh new nappy,
Mom and Dad just can't keep up, seven little stinkers,
Poopers and tinklers, seven tantrum-throwers,
Hoping for a kiss when your sister knocks you over,
Need that owee plastered,
Step aside, you bastard!
Scrapped like cats, but made up faster,
That's our babyhood: gleeful disaster.

Daddy works till he can't walk, one day calls us round to talk.
Says "Kids, take a look to your left and your right. This is your
tribe for the rest of your life. From the cradle to the grave,
these are your people, and that's all you have."
Then he passed, and life got nasty.

BERNIE: The little bit we got has got to last.

CHARLEY: Ma, she takes a downturn fast. She gives up now,
up to us now.

DELTA: We head off to kindergart, seven little broken hearts.

Alfa says "Remember Dad. We stay one locked-in crew."
So that's just what we do. Eat paste and stick like glue.

DAR: I sense this story has a sad direction,
Yet I can't help but envy that affection.

DION: The palace where I lived was rather cold,
We bowed and curtseyed, did what we were told.

DAR: That's too familiar; I know what you mean.
I grew up well behaved and crisp and clean.

DION: A little bit of mess looks really fun!

DAR: A crowd to run around with!

(They notice everyone staring.)

DION: *(To Alfa:)* Carry on.

ALFA: Roll through school and turn eighteen. Then something we have never seen. A fancy envelope comes in the mail, not stopped by rain or sleet or hail.

BERNIE: *(Quotes the letter, sounding like a pompous old man.)* "Congratulations! You've reached your majority. Time to sign up, line up, register to do your duty. No two ways, get on downtown today."

CHARLEY: Who's it for?

BERNIE: We can't tell. Seems to be for everyone.

DELTA: Just like how Aunt Lenore used to send us one birthday card every year. And on Christmas? One sweater.

ERNIE: OK, forget her. Stick to the story. How we got the letter,
Have to go and register.

CHARLEY: Who should go?

DELTA: I think you know!

BERNIE: Delta's on it. Let her.

ALL: In the Christmas sweater!

ERNIE: And she signed us up with her worst handwriting.

CHARLEY: Secret weapon all our lives. Saved our little butts from anything frightening.

ALFA: Class we don't want to take:
Art and woodshop
Subjects you want to drop —

BERNIE: Music

CHARLEY: Biology

DELTA: Culture Anthropology.

ERNIE: Chemistry or Western Lit,

DELTA: "Don't even worry. I'll deal with it."
Not to mention
detention
homework forgotten
lunches rotten in a locker bottom
gym clothes not washed
shoes not polished
library books somehow demolished...

ALFA: Delta writes a note in illegible scratches, nobody catches, turns it in *for* us:

DELTA: "Please excuse from Chorus. Ernie's got the stomach flu. Farley's down with something, too."

BERNIE: Now we send her down to the city center. Next to no time, Delta's back, puffed up big, and braggin' like a smokestack:

DELTA: No one could read that! Loop de loops and dashes, Xses and slashes. Shoulda seen the signature, gonna hurt their eyes for sure.
You know I signed a D for me, a C for Charley, F for Farley... All nice and smashed up. Nothing but a mash-up.   .

BERNIE: She wasn't so careful with the address, though. Wrote that pretty clearly.

CHARLEY: Didn't mean to.

DELTA: Cost us dearly.

CHARLEY: And the war went on, because war is war, and six months later, there's the door:

> *(Delta catches Greg's eye, swiftly pantomimes making a peanut butter sandwich. Bernie and Charley swing him into place and hand him the sandwich.)*

> *(Farley knocks on an imagined door. Greg answers, mouth full of food, and just barely keeping up.)*

GREG: MWELLO?

FARLEY: *(As a military rep, Southern crew-cut type:)* Greetings! Are you *(Reading from a paper:)* DAK-A-FEB BY-ROYT?

GREG: Mmmm...hmmm.

> *(Farley shoves a pack and big stick at Greg.)*

FARLEY: Report in the morning, soldier. Oh-six-thirty.

GREG: Nuh?

ALFA: Nothing about that sounded right.

BERNIE: The only six-thirty we know is at night. Never been up at *oh*-six-thirty since we were making our diapers dirty.

CHARLEY: And we're peaceful, mostly. Not harm-doers or evil-wishers. It's just not our way.

DELTA: We got in our fair share of scrapes but never fighting.

ERNIE: *Never* fighting. Alfa wouldn't have it. Don't disturb our Ma. If we scrapped in our room it was

ALFA: DOWNSTAIRS!

ERNIE: If we scuffled downstairs, it was

ALFA: OUTSIDE!

ERNIE: If we brawled in the yard, it was

ALL: TO THE PARK!

ALFA: And in the park, well, we didn't fight. More like putting on a show, you know.
The splendid seven. We each had our thing.

GREG: Alfa's tops at brainwork. And speaking up for all of us.

ALFA: Bernie does the Tai Chi. Connects to the ground, can't be knocked down.

BERNIE: Charley's strong as steel. He'd let the kiddies poke his muscles, twenty cents a feel.

CHARLEY: Delta's our swimmer.

DELTA: Ernie's crazy limber.

ERNIE: Farley's fast. He's mighty with the track skills.

FARLEY: Greg's special gift? The man can sit *still*.

BERNIE: We'd each take a turn, with Alfa announcing. No tussling or trouncing. Other kids? Our audience! There we were, our own little circus. What's to fight, what's to fuss? Not a nasty bone in all of us.

CHARLEY: Soldiering, we'd be the worst.
We don't want to kill.

"Hey, no, totally, go ahead.
You take that nice piece of land.
And practice your religion however you want it.
We don't need to hate or educate you on it."

DION: If ever I were crowned to lead a nation,
That tolerance would be my firm foundation.
A ruler should encourage a strong state
Without creating enemies to bait.

DAR: Huh, look at that! On one thing we're agreed.
"Live and let live" would be my country's creed.

CHARLEY: *(Grinning:)* You got it, friends, no need to make issues, never wish you harm or want to give you grief. So Greg tells this sergeant:

GREG: Hold up a sec, 'cause you're in for a surprise.
Fighting and so on, that's just not my size.
I'm a lover, like they say, a helmet wouldn't suit me.
If anything, let's sit around and talk it through, see?
And get down to the bottom of the reason why there's fighting.
You know down deep it's 'cause life can be frightening.
He holds on to what he's got, afraid *she's* got her eye on it.
And then *we* grab a little more, and that's what makes *them* violent.
Soon everybody's clutching, and they won't give up an inch.
Then you got an all-out war, everybody feels the pinch.
So keep your boots and bayonet
Let me get
Some lemonade. We'll sit in the shade, tell stories, make some rhymes.
You'll have a better time
Than trying to make a soldier
Like I told ya, if you knew me,

You'd soon see it's the wrong tree
For barking up. Let's lift a cup.

FARLEY: *(As Sergeant:)* Oh-six-thirty. I *know* you heard me.

ALFA: We all come home from a long day out. No jobs to be had, but we've been looking.
"Hey, where's Greg? And dinner's not cooking. What's up with that?"

ERNIE: I give a holler, look to see if he's out back.
And there's our man Greg, you never seen such a sad sack.

GREG: You won't believe it, I've just had the worst fright,
The military's called me and I'm leaving at the first light.

ERNIE: What? You'll never pull a trigger.
Couldn't, even if they shot you.

GREG: Don't know how I'll do it, but the man says I've got to.

ERNIE: We ought to tell Ma, but we don't have the heart.
Greg is her favorite, she'll take it too hard.
We sit up all night hugging, holding each other near,
Till five a.m. when Alfie says

ALFA: I've got an idea.
What happens if you don't show up?

GREG: He says they'll drag me down there.

ALFA: So let them come. But when they do,
Bernie will stand there instead of you.

GREG: What? No way.

ALFA: And when they try to grab you, Bernie, what'll you say?

BERNIE: *(Grounding in a martial arts stance:)* Go ahead. I'm sure it's not hard, with three against one.

Go on, put your back into it, this'll be fun.

CHARLEY: And they'll push and they'll shove like the wolf in the story,
Try to blow Bernie down and get nowhere for it.

ALFA: And the next thing that happens, if I'm guessing correct,
The sergeant's annoyed, says,

FARLEY: *(As Sergeant:)* Hey, the Selective
Service is no joke, this isn't no horsing.
We'll come back tomorrow with swords and we'll force ya.
This is what the world does with children in their prime.
Raise 'em to start killing. Best get willing. It's your time.
Tomorrow when we come again, we'll bring our sharp knives.
That'll be the end, unless you got nine lives.

GREG: No! I won't hear it. Then Bernie gets hurt!
You think this is helping? You're making it worse.
They come back with swords and they cut Bernie's heart out?

BERNIE: Naw, something tells me Alf's gone and figured that part out.

ALFA: You know I have, take a breath and hear me out,
'Cause the very next day, they're back with a shout,
Gonna teach a lesson to someone they couldn't move,
Can't drag ya outta there, what else can they do?
They've sharpened their blades, getting ready for war,
And then they show up, and who comes to the door?
It's Charley who greets them, perhaps even shirtless.
No matter what knives they bring, nothing could hurt less
For Charles, with his muscles and sinews and such,
There's just something in him that metal can't touch.

CHARLEY: And they'll assume I'm Bernie, see, that's the story, innit?

GREG: I'm getting it now — just took me a minute.

CHARLEY: Sure, bring 'em on, they can't cut me.
The whole muckin' army's not strong enough. But...

FARLEY: *(As Sergeant:)* Hey, what is this nonsense? You're stronger than steel?
Is that your game? Then here's the deal —
You come with us willing, and do your killing, or if you won't play nice,
Since we can't slice or drag ya,
I'll convince you what you oughta
With a board and some water.
It's plenty persuasive, I've used it real often,
You'll see when you're chokin' and coughin', I'll bet you.
One way or another, no question, we'll get you.
Respect to your mother.

GREG: No! Charley can't swim. It's never been his thing.
Just stands there with those wings on
When we go to the pool,
No, this isn't cool, Alf. I've got to go
Let the army know I'm theirs.
Just don't let Charley get wet or scared.

ALFA: *(Gently:)* Greg was never the best at school,
Not the brightest bulb or the sharpest tool.
Sweet and good, but you wouldn't call him quick.

FARLEY: You know how every kid makes that wicked discovery that there's no Santa, and they gotta tell the others? When we were nine —

ALFA: Eight.

FARLEY: Alf couldn't wait
Once she figured it out,

Had to shout:

ALFA: "You're gonna need to hear this,
Get on over here, kids!"

CHARLEY: We all come at a run. Alf says

ALFA: "It's been fun,
and I'm sorry to break it,
But Santa's not real. He's totally fake."
Bernie and Charley start crying, see?

DELTA: And Ernie says

ERNIE: "I knew it! It had to be!"
And Farley says

FARLEY: "Bogus? That's hilarious. HA!"
And Greg says,

GREG: "OK. But please don't tell Ma.
She'd be so disappoint—. Oh."

ALL EXCEPT GREG: Yeah.

GREG: Ah.

BERNIE: So that's our Greg. Not a step ahead,
That's not his style,
So it took him a while
to catch our drift. But we stuck with it:

DELTA: Greg, honey, focus now, who's the best swimmer?

GREG: Sure, that's you, Delta.
Fastest in the water, you're basically a fish.

DELTA: So if agua's the issue,
Who would you wish to
Throw in there for swimming, splashing and splishing?

GREG: Nobody but you. Breathing like a Chinook

when they come for good old Chuck.
Is that what you're thinking?

DELTA: I'm floating, not sinking.

(Farley [as Sergeant] and Delta perform a stylized version of water-boarding: repeated dunking interspersed with Farley's next lines.)

FARLEY: *(As Sergeant:)* You stinking draft-dodger. I swear now, just quit it.
You don't want to tick me off, 'cause that won't be pretty.

DELTA: Yeah, I believe you.

FARLEY: *(As Sergeant:)* I'm gonna leave you one more time
You may be tops at strength and skilled at water-breathing,
But now I'm seething. No more Mister Nice Guy.
Kiss your family goodbye.
Then show up in the morning like I said
Or, swear to god, you'll hang till you're dead.

GREG: *(Panicked:)* Delta, no!

DELTA: Stick with us, now.

GREG: Somebody...will take your place. But who, what, how?

ERNIE: Who's got a neck that goes all the way down?
Remember when we used to play cowboys and crooks?
The sheriff would ride in —

DAR: Which one would that be?

BERNIE: Usually me —
"You took my horse, you no-good egg-sucker."

ERNIE: "You got me mixed up with some other mucker."

BERNIE: "Nope. Hang him high, boys, till he 'sphixiates,
If there's anything I hate it's a low-down horse-grabber,

aw, yeah, but we nabbed ya. Rope him up from that tree!"

ERNIE: Which is what you'd do to me.
Then you see I'd stretch from the shoulders to the chin,
give you all a grin,
attenuate, elongulate, and
"Later, hater, I'm not a suffocater."

GREG: Ernie, you bet! You'd start hung up high,
Say "I ain't dead yet," then you'd make a funny face,
twitch a little this way, tweak a little that way,
and wouldn't you know, pretty soon your toes
would be ticklin' the blacktop.
Right there by the backstop.

ERNIE: Kids would get to playing ball
Forgetting me. And I'd get comfy,
Take a little nap
Till the sheriff came back.

BERNIE: "What's this I see? Hot dang, you got the best of me."

ERNIE: You'd undo that big knot,
Then we'd trot off to lunch, right?

    (All trot.)

I mean that was fun, right?
Greggy, now you follow?

DELTA: Sergeant comes tomorrow
Tries his best to hang our E.
But Ernie can't be hanged, ya see.

ALFA: And everything happened just like we planned it.
Sarge gets mad and madder, doesn't understand it.
Gives up on Ernie, that's Day Five.

DION: Good so far! Everyone's alive.

DAR: Until?

ERNIE: We hear that voice again:

FARLEY: "Now you've gone and done it, made me lose my temper,
Didn't step up and do what you should have.
No more time to scam it, damn it.
Next time you see me, it's with a big old semi-
automatic weapon. That's what I'll pack.
Know it for a fact.
You'll come with me, or one two three:
a bullet so fast you won't even see it."

GREG: *(Upbeat:)* Great! Now what, gang, fill me in, let me have it.
What do we do to prevent a tragedy?
Farley's fast, but he can't outrun a gun.
Ernie's nice and stretchy, and that can be impressive,
But Ern can't dodge a bullet or stretch out of its way.
Delta is a water wiz, but not even her crawl
Can save her from that fall.
Charley's tougher than a blade,
He can't be chopped by metal,
But put him in the line of fire, he's just as dead as dead.
And sure we know that Bernie's tops at never falling over,
But shoot her with a pistol, right away she's pushing clover.
Alf, you got a secret plan that'll get us out of this mess?
I know you do. *We've come so far.*

(Everybody looks to Alfa, shifting so that Alfa and Farley stand facing off in the center of a circle. The Seven now realize they are out of options.)

ALFA: We left that second. And here we are.

(A silence, broken by Queenie.)

QUEENIE: It isn't our fault, you guys, really.
They shouldn't have come to the valley.
We've barely enough
Food and water and stuff,
To add seven more would be folly.

CONSTANCE: It's just not sustainable. We can't all starve just to help out some people we — no offense — don't even know.

CORNELIUS: We feel for you, of course we do, but we got here first.

ALFA: End of the line, gang. That's Game Over.

BERNIE: Got no cover. We're out on the ice.

CHARLEY: Hang or drown or sliced by a blade,

DELTA: Nothing else made us turn and run,

ERNIE: But now we go back and face the gun.

FARLEY: I'll take the bullet, guys, let me do it.

(All look at each other.)

GREG: There's none of us could live with that. There's only one way we go back.

ALFA: Together, then.

BERNIE: And all for one.

CHARLEY: We go down together, in death as in life.

DELTA: Thank you for listening, all the same.

ERNIE: We do understand, name of the game.
Resources being what they are.

FARLEY: Only so far the food can stretch.

GREG: It was nice to meet you, and we wish you the best.

DION AND DAR: Wait!

(They look at each other.)

TREY: Please, don't drag this out.

CONSTANCE: They've made their peace, and we've made our choice.

CORNELIUS: I'm sure we all feel terrible enough.

DION: What if there's another way? *(To Dar:)* I happen to know of these kingdoms.

(Dar flies to him.)

Could you put up with me for fifty years despite
Not feeling anything?

DAR: Uh-huh. All right.
(To All:) My fiancé and I are going home.
To share our lives and join our crowns and thrones.
There's space, and peace, and food enough for you,
Or will be when the ceremony's through.

DION: Although our families' planning this was bad,
It's not the worst idea they ever had.
(Teasing:) I'm reconciled to this awful match.

DAR: And some would say you're actually a catch.
And with the wealth we stumbled on through birth,
We can help those whose luck is somewhat worse.
We'll run home now and open up the gates,
And welcome you. A cheerful future waits.

QUINN: But what about the punishment you threatened?

DION: Forget that now. A brighter future beckons.
You party animals can be our guards
And keep the spies and meddlers from our yard.
Go on ahead and have them make a feast.

For—well—a dozen hungry mouths at least!

(The Qs cheer, exit.)

DAR: *(To Constance, Cornelius, and Trey:)* You'll come with us as well, I hope, you three.
You'll get your old jobs back. Leave that to me.
(To Constance and Cornelius:) You'll live away from him, a private street.
Secluded so your paths will never meet.
Soon Spring will come reward you for your patience,
And bring you other dreams and aspirations.

CONSTANCE: If you don't mind, Your Highnesses,

CORNELIUS: we think we'll take our chances

TREY: roaming the earth

CONSTANCE: never to meet again.

(They exit: Constance and Cornelius together; Trey hesitates, then follows them.)

(Alfa and company have been picking up their things and lining up, except for Greg, who is not paying attention.)

(Bernie, Charley, Delta, Ernie, Farley exit quickly; Alfa remains to say goodbye to Dion and Dar.)

ALFA: You won't regret this.

DAR: We already don't.

(Alfa embraces or shakes hands with Dar and Dion, takes Greg with her when she exits.)

(Dion spots Erdos.)

DION: And you, my friend, don't think we'll leave you here!

ERDOS: With due respect, Your Grace, I'll disappear.
It's like I told you, I enjoy the quiet.

DION: But now and then, right? Not a steady diet!

DAR: Just let him be, sweetheart. I think he means it.

ERDOS: See there? You'll learn to listen to your Queen.

(Dion and Dar wave a final goodbye to Erdos and exit.)

A single sigh.
A perfect plum.
Some things are just right
Without another one.

Some numbers irreducible,
So clean and bright and prime.

(Looking in the direction where the others have left:) Some people irreplaceable.
Like words that have no rhyme.

(He pulls up one leg and stands like a stork.)

(End of play.)

The Author Speaks

What inspired you to write this play?
When Wilson High School in Portland, Oregon, invited me to write for their excellent drama program, they gave me one limitation: all of the characters must be roughly the same age as the actors; no 15-year-olds playing senators or stockbrokers. While I value this choice both as an artist and as an educator, facing it as a playwright felt like a real challenge! How to leave out teachers, parents, and older or younger siblings, without their absence feeling somewhat artificial?

The word that came to mind was "escape." My imagination began to play in a green world away from authority figures and everyday obligations, the world where Shakespeare's hardiest young characters find refuge, find love, find themselves. The resonance with Shakespeare then prompted me to think about writing in verse, an ambition that had been hovering in the back of my writer's brain for years.

What were the biggest challenges involved in the writing of this play?
Once I had the notion to write in verse, I couldn't shake it off, but I was intimidated at the same time. The first few writing sessions, I had to tell myself "you can always go back to prose if this gets too hard!" But by the end of a week I'd started to find my way.

I'm also not used to writing for large casts! These days, playwrights are so often asked to keep cast size down to four or five. Writing for a cast of 18 was thrilling but also a challenge.

What are the most common mistakes that occur in productions of your work?

What a great question! My plays seem to be tricky in terms of tone. I've seen productions of a couple of my plays where everything was right, beat by beat, but the tone was almost the opposite of what I'd had in mind. Generally, the stories I write are about good, clever, and loving people who are failing each other in various ways—not about stupid or cruel people. In *Prime*, for example, Cornelius and Constance mean the world to each other, and when they are at odds for the first time in their lives, they find it disorienting and painful. Trey is a genuinely good guy with good intentions, not an intentional manipulator. Dion and Dar bicker but they also have deep tenderness toward each other—even when they don't know it.

How did you research the subject?

There's a cool book called *A Beginner's Guide to Constructing the Universe* that's about the cultural significance of different numbers. I love that book and went through it again for *Prime*. And I did quite a lot of reading on number theory and number theorists, which taught me that prime numbers to them are like favorite colors or flavors to me, or like jokes or music. That started to give me a handle on the Erdos character.

Beyond that, I caught up on a few folktales. Readers may recognize the storyline of the Seven from *Anansi the Spider* or a similar story I grew up with called *The Seven Chinese Brothers*. I had a creepy fascination with that story in childhood, and always thought I might dig into it as a playwright someday, so I spent some time with variations of it, and of the dancing princesses story. Then I put them aside and just started playing.

Are any characters modeled after real life or historical figures?

Erdos is named for a real-life and very quirky mathematician, Paul Erdos. The Erdos of our play is not really modeled after him, but it's a tip of the hat. The math world is full of funny and odd stories about him, and you get the impression of somebody really swimming outside mainstream life, never settled anywhere, just kind of flying around fueled by his work. Our Erdos isn't quite like that, but he's certainly an outsider.

Shakespeare gave advice to the players in *Hamlet*; if you could give advice to your cast what would it be?

The various forms of verse in *Prime* can be thought of as languages that belong to lands or cultures that border each other. In many parts of the world, including parts of the U.S., it's not unusual to hear multiple languages on the street, or for people to switch in and out of different languages as they encounter different people. I think the verse forms work in a similar way here. And often, the meter and rhyme scheme of a particular conversation is determined by who is dominant in that interaction, or who is driving the scene. My advice would be that all this may come to you intuitively as you dive in; trust it!

How was the first production different from the vision that you created in your mind?

The first production was pretty sublime. Director Matt Zrebski wrote some great music for the Qs' dance sections, and worked with them to devise funny, scary dance sequences. Those were fully developed to an extent I didn't expect and really loved (though you could also do them more simply). I also realized what a tricky bit of writing I'd created for the love triangle—all that quick switching of directions! But once the actors got hold of that, it was really satisfying.

There was one performance when a cast member's young siblings were in the house, and as we headed into the Santa Claus section, I suddenly felt myself turning purple with concerns for those little ones. I didn't want to ruin anybody's Christmas, and I've never felt so protective of specific audience members! As it happened, they didn't seem to have any big reaction, but I stand by the recommendation of this show for middle school ages and up.

Finally, I really enjoyed how the actors immediately started hanging out with their onstage tribes during breaks, sitting together for notes, and so on. I would love to hear from other groups that produce this show to see if that goes with the territory!

About the Author

Ellen Margolis is a founding member of Playwrights West in Portland, Oregon. Her plays, which have been produced at theatres and festivals throughout the United States, include *Calumnies, American Soil, Splasher, What We Thought*, and *A Little Chatter*, which appears in a collection of baseball plays from Playscripts, Inc. She has received commissions from Portland Shakespeare Project, Mile Square Theatre, Shaking-the-Tree Studio, and the Susan G. Komen Foundation. Excerpts from her plays can be seen in the *Audition Arsenal* series, published by Smith & Kraus. She is also the editor of *Singular Voices*, a book of monologues from the International Centre for Women Playwrights. Her work has been recognized by the Portland Civic Theatre Guild, the New York International Fringe Festival, the Trustus Foundation, the Jane Chambers Competition, and the National 10-Minute Play Contest. She teaches at Pacific University in Oregon, and also works as a director and dialect coach.

About YouthPLAYS

YouthPLAYS (www.youthplays.com) is a publisher of award-winning professional dramatists and talented new discoveries, each with an original theatrical voice, and all dedicated to expanding the vocabulary of theatre for young actors and audiences. On our website you'll find one-act and full-length plays and musicals for teen and pre-teen (and even college) actors, as well as duets and monologues for competition. Many of our authors' works have been widely produced at high schools and middle schools, youth theatres and other TYA companies, both amateur and professional, as well as at elementary schools, camps, churches and other institutions serving young audiences and/or actors worldwide. Most are intended for performance by young people, while some are intended for adult actors performing for young audiences.

YouthPLAYS was co-founded by professional playwrights Jonathan Dorf and Ed Shockley. It began merely as an additional outlet to market their own works, which included a substantial body of award-winning published and unpublished plays and musicals. Those interested in their published plays were directed to the respective publishers' websites, and unpublished plays were made available in electronic form. But when they saw the desperate need for material for young actors and audiences—coupled with their experience that numerous quality plays for young people weren't finding a home—they made the decision to represent the work of other playwrights as well. Dozens and dozens of authors are now members of the YouthPLAYS family, with scripts available both electronically and in traditional acting editions. We continue to grow as we look for exciting and challenging plays and musicals for young actors and audiences.

About ProduceaPlay.com

Let's put up a play! Great idea! But producing a play takes time, energy and knowledge. While finding the necessary time and energy is up to you, ProduceaPlay.com is a website designed to assist you with that third element: knowledge.

Created by YouthPLAYS' co-founders, Jonathan Dorf and Ed Shockley, ProduceaPlay.com serves as a resource for producers at all levels as it addresses the many facets of production. As Dorf and Shockley speak from their years of experience (as playwrights, producers, directors and more), they are joined by a group of award-winning theatre professionals and experienced teachers from the world of academic theatre, all making their expertise available for free in the hope of helping this and future generations of producers, whether it's at the school or university level, or in community or professional theatres.

The site is organized into a series of major topics, each of which has its own page that delves into the subject in detail, offering suggestions and links for further information. For example, Publicity covers everything from Publicizing Auditions to How to Use Social Media to Posters to whether it's worth hiring a publicist. Casting details Where to Find the Actors, How to Evaluate a Resume, Callbacks and even Dealing with Problem Actors. You'll find guidance on your Production Timeline, The Theater Space, Picking a Play, Budget, Contracts, Rehearsing the Play, The Program, House Management, Backstage, and many other important subjects.

The site is constantly under construction, so visit often for the latest insights on play producing, and let it help make your play production dreams a reality.

More from YouthPLAYS

Rumors of Polar Bears by Jonathan Dorf
Dramedy. 90-100 minutes. 8-25+ females, 4-15+ males (14-40+ performers possible).

A ragtag band of teens hits the road to survive a climate induced catastrophe. As they encounter unfinished coloring books, failing paradises, a frozen-in-time former pre-kindergarten drama class, bikers determined to turn the chaos into their new world order, and a mysterious people that even the bikers won't cross, will the refugees follow Deme and chase after the rumored polar bears that she believes are the key to their survival, or will their patchwork family fall apart?

HKFN: The Abbreviated Adventures of Huckleberry Finn by Jeff Goode
Comedy. 25-35 minutes. 3-8 females, 2-6 males (5-10 performers possible).

The actor playing Huck flees a production of Twain's controversial classic. But when the actor who plays Jim runs away too and troublemakers Duke & King join in, their fugitive theatre company launches into a series of misadventures—while domineering Aunt Polly tries to force them back into the "real" play. In the chaos, that play—and its discussion about race—may be happening without them knowing it.

Dancing With Myself by Leanne Griffin
Dramedy. 35-45 minutes. 7 females.

Goth Girl. Moody Chick. Gamer. Cheerleader. New Kid. Jock. Nerd. Seven high school girls and the labels they're forced to wear. But whether it's sports or a sleepover or the classroom or a school dance or the ups and downs of daily life, they'll use music as their inspiration to break free of the stereotypes and discover the unique identity they each possess.

The Superhero Ultraferno by Don Zolidis
Comedy. 100-110 minutes. 6-50 females, 6-50 males (12-90+ performers).

Now that nerds have taken over the world, it's imperative that all popular kids learn everything they can about comic book superheroes. Join two nerds and a crack team of actors as they race hilariously through the world of tights-wearing crimefighters, from the 1960s TV Batman to the soap opera insanity of the Fantastic Four to a bizarre, German opera of Spiderman. Also available as a one-act.

The Ghost Moments by Randy Wyatt
Drama. 45-70 minutes. 1-10 females, 1-5 males (2-15 performers total).

We all have ghosts that haunt us. Some are literal: Matty tries to rid his sister's apartment of a spirit that may or may not be there, Zachary prepares his bunker for the zombie apocalypse. Others are metaphorical: Marianne's absent father, Caroline's memories of water, Carver's secret powers. As we witness hauntings and exorcisms through a series of monologues, this group of characters and their loves, longings, joy and pain, will haunt us long after the curtain falls.

Jennifer the Unspecial: Time Travel, Love Potions & 8th Grade by Matthew Mezzacappa (book & lyrics) & Cynthia Chi-Wing Wong (music)
Musical. 90 minutes. 5-30 males, 3-30 females (8-60 performers possible).

When her science teacher's invention goes horribly wrong, awkward, clumsy eighth grader Jennifer finds herself thrust into a time-traveling adventure with three of her classmates. Through the journey, as they encounter warriors, artists, presidents and love potions, Jennifer discovers she doesn't need anyone's approval to be absolutely amazing and special.

Mi Coche, Mi Quince by Susan Lieberman

Dramedy. 95-110 minutes. 5-12+ females, 3-8+ males (8-20+ performers possible).

High school senior Luis, pillar of his fractured Mexican-American family, is set to play a key role in his sister Ana's upcoming quinceañera. But when his girlfriend Miriam learns she's pregnant, Luis' future plans and Ana's *quince* dreams are derailed. As Miriam explores adoption, challenging the cultural conventions of their community and Luis' commitment to the relationship, Ana's traditional rite of passage may just become a time of unexpected transformation for everyone.

The Exceptional Childhood Center by Dylan Schifrin

Comedy. 25-35 minutes. 2-4 females, 2-3 males (5-6 performers possible).

Reggie Watson has been accepted into the right preschool. He's set for life...as long as he can make it through the one-day trial period. But when desperation breeds disaster and his future hangs in the balance, Reggie and his band of quirky classmates may just discover things about themselves that school could never teach them.

Choose Your Own Oz by Tommy Jamerson

Comedy. 85-100 minutes. 4-15+ females, 4-15+ males (10-30+ performers possible).

The Wizard of Oz meets *Choose Your Own Adventure* in this fresh and fast-paced retelling of the L. Frank Baum classic in which the audience plays playwright and gets the chance to change everything from Dorothy's footwear (silver slippers or ruby red...clown shoes?) to Toto's species (lion, tiger or octopus?—oh my!) to the Witch's flying footmen. A delight for children of all ages, **Choose Your Own Oz** reminds us all that at the end of the day, there really is no place like home.

Made in the USA
Charleston, SC
15 January 2016